www.sachildrensbooks.com
Copyright©2015 by S.A. Publishing
innans@gmail.com

All rights reserved. No part of this book may be reproduced in any form or by any electronic or mechanical means, including information storage and retrieval systems, without written permission from the publisher or author, except in the case of a reviewer, who may quote brief passages embodied in critical articles or in a review. Alle Rechte vorbehalten. Kein Teil dieses Buches darf in irgendeiner Form oder durch irgendwelche elektronischen oder mechanischen Mitteln, einschließlich Informationen Regalbediengeräte schriftlich beim Verlag, mit Ausnahme von einem Rezensenten, kurze Passagen in einer Bewertung zitieren darf reproduziert, ohne Erlaubnis.

First edition, 2016
Translated from English by Tess Parthum
Aus dem Englischen übersetzt von Tess Parthum

Boxer and Brandon (German English Bilingual Edition)
ISBN: 978-1-5259-0131-7 paperback
ISBN: 978-1-5259-0132-4 hardcover
ISBN: 978-1-5259-0130-0 eBook

Although the author and the publisher have made every effort to ensure the accuracy and completeness of information contained in this book, we assume no responsibility for errors , inaccuracies, omission, inconsistency, or consequences from such information.

Please note that the German and English versions of the story have been written to be as close as possible. However, in some cases they differ in order to accommodate nuances and fluidity of each language.

Inna Nusinsky

Illustrationen von Gillian Tolentino
Illustrations by Gillian Tolentino

Hallo, ich heiße Boxer. Ich bin ein Boxer. Ich gehöre zu einer Hunderasse, die sich Boxer nennt. Es freut mich, dich kennenzulernen! Diese Geschichte erzählt, wie ich zu meiner neuen Familie kam.

Hello, my name is Boxer. I'm a boxer. I'm a type of dog called a boxer. Nice to meet you! This is the story of how I got my new family.

Alles begann, als ich 2 Jahre alt war.
It all started when I was two years old.

Ich hatte kein Zuhause. Ich lebte auf der Straße und fraß aus Mülltonnen. Die Menschen wurden ziemlich wütend auf mich, wenn ich ihre Mülltonnen umwarf.
I was homeless. I lived on the street and ate out of garbage cans. People got pretty mad at me when I knocked over their trash cans.

„Verschwinde von hier!", schrien sie. Manchmal musste ich sehr schnell wegrennen!
"Get out of here!" they would shout. Sometimes I had to run away really fast!

Das Leben in der Stadt kann hart sein.
Living in the city can be hard.

Wenn ich nicht gerade auf Futtersuche war, saß ich gern da und beobachtete die Menschen, die auf dem Gehweg vorbeikamen.

When I wasn't looking for food, I liked to sit and watch people walk by on the sidewalk.

Manchmal sah ich die Leute mit meinen traurigen Augen an und sie gaben mir Futter.

Sometimes, I would look at people with my sad eyes and they would give me food.

„Oh, was für ein süßes Hündchen! Hier hast du einen Snack", sagten sie.

"Oh, what a cute doggy! Here, have a snack," they would say.

„Brandon, füttere diesen Hund nicht! Er wird nur noch mehr haben wollen", rief sein Papa. Brandon zog das Sandwich weg.

"Brandon, don't feed that dog! He'll just come looking for more," exclaimed his dad. Brandon pulled the sandwich back.

So nah—ich konnte die Butter riechen! Eltern wollen niemals mit mir teilen!

So close—I could smell the peanut butter! Parents never want to share with me!

Ich winselte so jämmerlich ich konnte, als sie fortgingen.

I whined as pitifully as I could as they walked away.

Danach beschloss ich, ein Nickerchen zu machen. Ich hatte gerade einen wunderschönen Traum.

After that, I decided to take a nap. I was having a wonderful dream.

Ich war in einem Park und alles bestand aus Fleisch! Die Bäume waren Steaks! Es war der beste]Traum, den ich jemals hatte.

I was in a park and everything was made from meat! The trees were steaks! It was the best dream ever.

Allerdings weckte mich etwas auf. Direkt vor mir lag ein Stück Sandwich! Ich sprang auf meine Pfoten und schlang es hinunter.

Something woke me up, though. Right in front of me was a piece of a sandwich! I jumped to my feet and gobbled it down.

Mhmmm! Es war so gut! Genau wie in meinem Traum.

Mmmmm! It was so good! Just like my dream.

„Schh", sagte Brandon. „Erzähl es nicht Papa." Was für ein netter kleiner Junge, dachte ich mir.

"Shhh," said Brandon. "Don't tell Dad." *What a nice little boy*, I thought to myself.

Tag für Tag kam Brandon mich besuchen und gab mir einen Snack. Eines Tages dann…

Day after day, Brandon would come visit me and give me a snack. Then, one day…

„Beeil dich, Brandon. Du wirst zu spät zur Schule kommen", sagte Brandons Papa.

"Hurry up, Brandon. You'll be late for school," said Brandon's dad.

„Ich komme!", schrie Brandon. Im Vorbeirennen fiel ihm eine braune Tüte auf den Gehweg.

"I'm coming!" shouted Brandon as he ran past, dropping a brown bag on the sidewalk.

Ich schnüffelte, lief hin und schaute hinein. Sie war voller Essen!

Sniffing around, I walked up to it and looked inside. It was full of food!

Ich wollte gerade alles auffressen, als mir ein Gedanke kam. Brandon bringt mir immer Futter, wenn ich Hunger habe. Wenn ich sein Essen fresse, dann wird er Hunger haben.

I was just about to eat it all when I thought of something. *Brandon always brings me food when I'm hungry. If I eat his food, then he'll be hungry.*

„Ich komme, Brandon!",
jaulte ich.

"I'm coming, Brandon!"
I howled.

Er und sein Vater waren schon weit die Straße hinunter. Ich rannte ihnen mit der braunen Tüte im Maul hinterher.

He and his dad were way down the street. I ran after them with the brown bag in my mouth.

Als ich an einer Gasse vorbeikam, sah ich eine Katze. Ich hasse Katzen! Ich vergaß meine Mission und ließ die Tüte fallen.

As I was passing an alleyway, I saw a cat. I hate cats! I forgot about my mission and dropped the bag.

„Wuff, verschwinde von hier, Katze!", bellte ich.

"Bark, get out of here, cat!" I barked.

Dann erinnerte ich mich an Brandons Mittagessen. Er würde Hunger haben, wenn ich ihm nicht sein Mittagessen brachte!

Then I remembered Brandon's lunch. He was going to be hungry if I didn't bring him his lunch!

Es war schwer, aber ich vergaß die Katze. Ich hob die braune Tüte wieder auf und rannte los.

It was hard, but I forgot about the cat. I picked up the brown bag again and started running.

Ein Stück weiter die Straße hinunter hielt ich erneut an. Eine Metzgerei!

Further down the street, I stopped again. A butcher shop!

Da hingen überall Fleischstücke und Würstchen. Mmmmmh...

There were pieces of meat and sausages hanging everywhere. Mmmmm...

Halt! Ich musste Brandon sein Mittagessen bringen oder er würde Hunger bekommen!

Wait! I had to bring Brandon his lunch or he was going to be hungry!

Es war schwer, aber ich vergaß das Fleisch. Ich schnappte mir das Mittagessen und rannte wieder los.

It was hard, but I forgot about the meat. I grabbed the lunch and started running again.

Ich bog um eine Ecke und hielt an. Da war ein anderer Hund, der mit seinem Schwanz wedelte.

I turned a corner and stopped. There was another dog wagging his tail.

„Hallo, möchtest du spielen?", bellte er.

"Hi, want to play?" he woofed.

„Klar möchte ich!", antwortete ich. „Aber warte, ich kann gerade nicht. Ich muss Brandon sein Mittagessen bringen."

"I sure do!" I answered. "Oh, wait, I can't right now. I have to bring Brandon his lunch."

Es war schwer, aber ich vergaß das Spielen. Ich schnappte mir das Essen und rannte wieder los.

It was hard, but I forgot about playing.
I grabbed the lunch and started running again.

Ich konnte die Schule sehen - und da war Brandon mit seinem Papa! Ich rannte, so schnell ich konnte.

I could see the school—and there was Brandon with his dad! I ran as fast as I could.

Ich blieb vor Brandon stehen und ließ sein Mittagessen auf den Gehweg fallen. Gerade rechtzeitig!

Stopping in front of Brandon, I dropped his lunch bag on the sidewalk.
Just in time!

„Schau mal, Papa, er hat mir mein Mittagessen gebracht!", rief Brandon.

"Look, Dad, he brought my lunch!" exclaimed Brandon.

„Toll, das hat er wirklich. Das ist erstaunlich!", sagte sein Papa. Beide streichelten meinen Kopf.

"Wow, he sure did. That's amazing!" said his dad. They both patted me on the head.

Brandon war glücklich und sein Papa auch.

Brandon was happy and so was his dad.

Sein Papa war sogar so glücklich, dass er mich mit nach Hause nahm. Er badete mich. Er gab mir Futter!

In fact, his dad was so happy that he brought me home. He gave me a bath. He gave me food!

Wenn Brandon und sein Papa nun spazieren gehen, darf ich mit ihnen spazieren gehen. Und wenn sie nach Hause gehen, darf ich mit ihnen nach Hause gehen!

Now when Brandon and his dad go walking, I get to walk with them. And when they go home, I get to go home with them!

Ich liebe mein neues Zuhause und meine neue Familie!

I love my new home and my new family!